Backyard Bugwatcher

Identifying and caring for New Zealand arthropods

By Robinne Weiss

The Bugmobile

Education on six legs

Bugs and Books

Backyard Bugwatcher

by Robinne Weiss

ISBN: 978-0-473-40379-9

Front cover photos (clockwise from top right): chorus cicada (*Amphipsalta zealandica*), yellow admiral butterfly pupa (*Vanessa itea*), New Zealand praying mantis (*Orthodera novaezealandiae*), katydid (*Caedicia simplex*)

Back cover photos (clockwise from top right): drone fly (*Eristalis tenax*), yellow admiral butterfly (*Vanessa itea*), burnt pine longhorn beetle (*Arhopalus tristis*), New Zealand praying mantis (*Orthodera novaezealandiae*)

Contents

Bug Basics

What is an Insect?

Insects are arthropods—animals with jointed legs and an exoskeleton. As adults, insects have six legs, three main body regions (head, thorax, and abdomen), and two antennae. Many adult insects also have two or four wings. Insects are the only arthropods with wings.

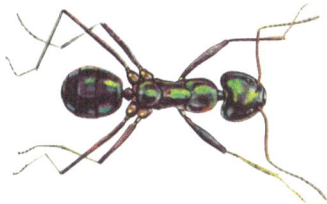

But, when it comes to arthropods, nothing is quite that simple. Some insects are legless, including many insect **larvae**; some larvae have extra leg-like appendages; and the distinctions between the three body regions are often difficult to see.

And if that wasn't enough confusion, some six-legged creatures with three main body regions and two antennae are not insects.

Insects belong to the class Hexapoda (meaning six-legged). Within this class, there are currently 31 orders. Three of those orders are considered non-insect Hexapods, and the remaining 28 are the insects.

The list of orders on the right includes all the insects known today, but this list is changing all the time. New discoveries can change the list dramatically, as our understanding of insects grows.

Scientists have identified about a million species of insect, but there are many more out there. In fact, there may be as many as 7.8 million species of insect on Earth.

As you can see, we have a lot to learn!

Non-Insect Hexapods
Protura—proturans
Diplura—diplurans
Collembola—springtails, snowfleas

Insects
Archaeognatha—bristletails
Zygentoma—silverfish, firebrats
Ephemeroptera—mayflies
Odonata—dragonflies, damselflies
Grylloblattodea—rock crawlers
Phasmatodea—walkingsticks, timemas
Orthoptera—grasshoppers, crickets, wētā
Mantodea—mantids
Blattodea—cockroaches, termites
Mantophasmatodea—gladiators (this order was discovered in 2002)
Dermaptera—earwigs
Embioptera—webspinners
Plecoptera—stoneflies
Zoraptera—angel insects
Psocodea—lice
Hemiptera—true bugs, cicadas, hoppers, psyllids, aphids, whiteflies, scales
Thysanoptera—thrips
Neuroptera—lacewings, antlions
Megaloptera—alderflies, dobsonflies
Raphidioptera—snakeflies
Coleoptera—beetles
Strepsiptera—twisted-wing parasites
Mecoptera—scorpionflies
Siphonaptera—fleas
Diptera—flies
Trichoptera—caddisflies
Lepidoptera—butterflies, moths
Hymenoptera—wasps, bees, ants, sawflies

Parts of an Insect

Antennae—detect smells, touch, sounds, and tastes.

Compound eyes—made of many individual **ommatidia**, each of which acts as an individual eye. Compound eyes cannot produce sharp, detailed images like our eyes do, but they are good at detecting motion—an important trait for fast-flying insects, or for avoiding predators and fly swatters.

Mouthparts—these vary wildly, from chewing mandibles in beetles, to scissor-like slicing mouthparts in horseflies, to straw-like mouthparts in moths and butterflies. Each type of mouthpart has evolved for a particular food source.

Ocelli—three small eyes on the top of the head. They help regulate the insect's daily rhythms.

Wings—Only adult insects have wings.

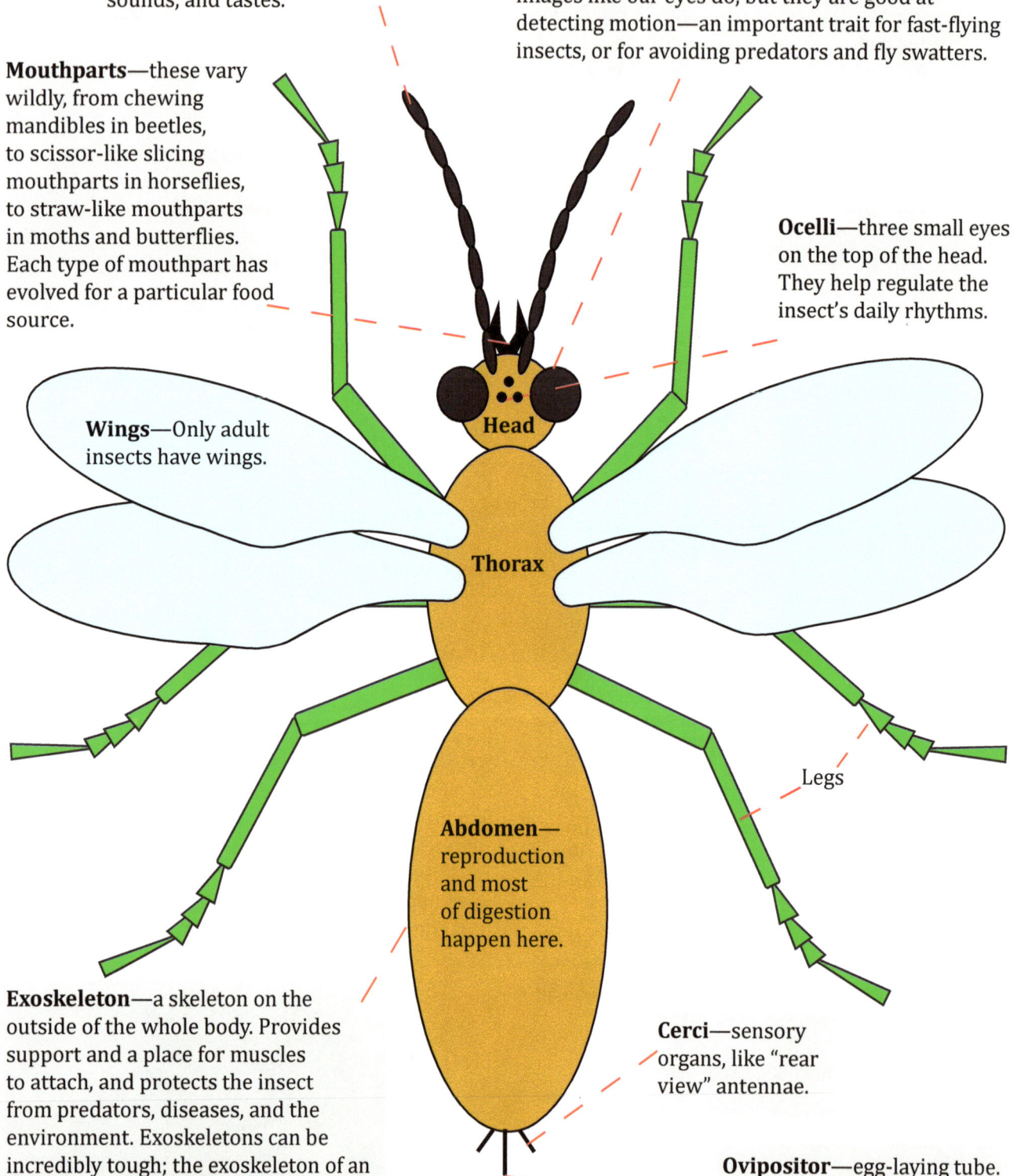

Head

Thorax

Legs

Abdomen—reproduction and most of digestion happen here.

Exoskeleton—a skeleton on the outside of the whole body. Provides support and a place for muscles to attach, and protects the insect from predators, diseases, and the environment. Exoskeletons can be incredibly tough; the exoskeleton of an insect's jaws (**mandibles**) can reach a hardness of 3 on Moh's scale of mineral hardness—the same as copper.

Cerci—sensory organs, like "rear view" antennae.

Ovipositor—egg-laying tube. Females only. Sometimes modified into a sting.

Inside an Insect

Blood—called **hemolymph**. It flows loosely around the insect's body cavity, not through blood vessels. Like our blood, hemolymph carries nutrients, hormones, wastes, and immune defences. Unlike our blood, however, insect hemolymph does not carry oxygen (except in a few species). Hemolymph is also sometimes used as a chemical defence against predators. Ladybugs, for example, have hemolymph that smells and tastes bad. When threatened, they bleed from their leg joints, giving a predator a nasty mouthful.

Heart—called the **dorsal aorta**. This muscular tube pumps the hemolymph (blood) around the body.

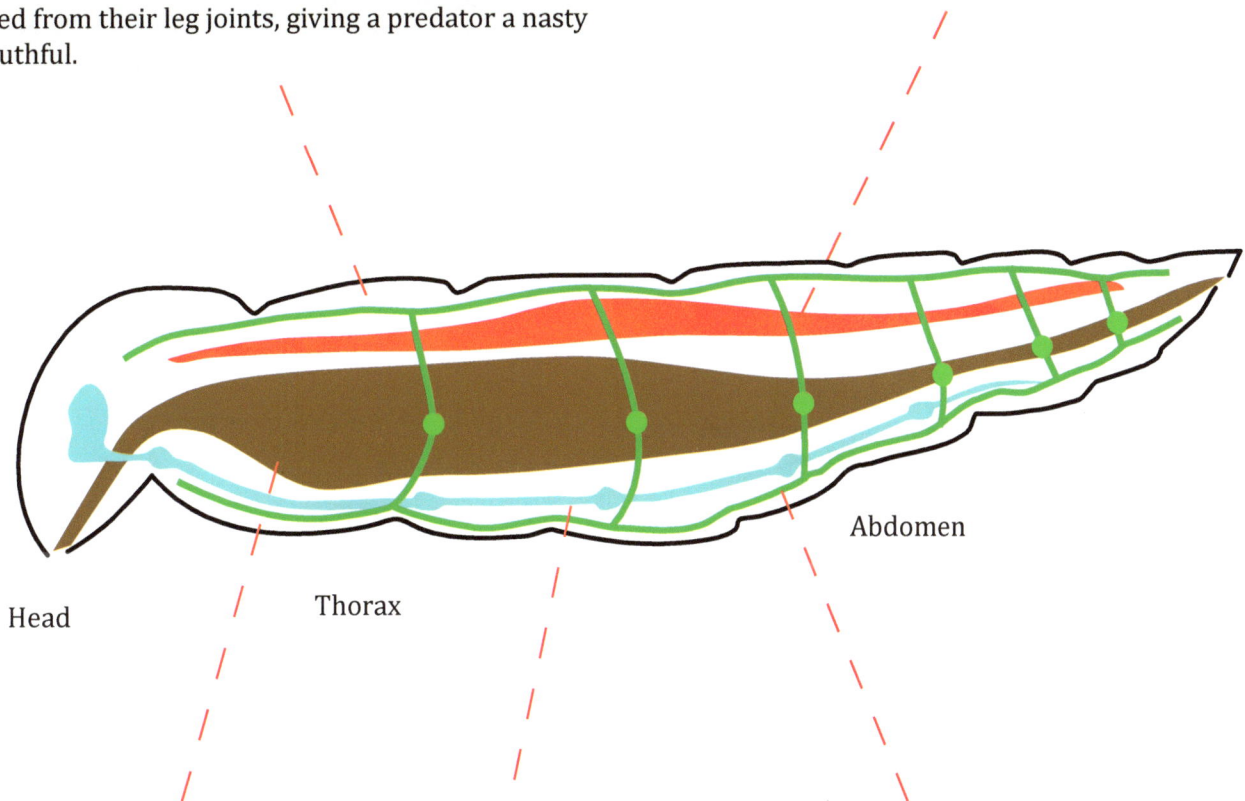

Head

Thorax

Abdomen

Gut—digests food, like your stomach and intestines.

Nervous system—the insect's central nerve cord runs down its belly. A brain in the head controls many functions. Small clusters of nerves along the central nerve cord, called **ganglia**, control legs and wings. Ganglia provide quick reflexes for getting away from predators.

Trachea—tubes that carry oxygen to all the cells in an insect's body. Holes in the abdomen (**spiracles**) lead to the trachea. Trachea are lined with exoskeleton, so when the insect moults the trachea shed a layer, too. You can often see the larger trachea in the shed exoskeletons of cicadas and other large insects—they look like white strings attached to the inside of the abdomen.

Life Cycle and Development

An insect's life span can range from a few days to seventeen years. Most insects in temperate regions, however, have a life span of a year. Some notable exceptions are some of our wētā, which may live up to eight or nine years; our native cicadas, which spend up to three years as nymphs underground; and on the other end of the spectrum, many of our aphid pests, which have a generation time of about five days.

Insects go through **metamorphosis**—a dramatic change in body shape—during their life cycle. There are two types of metamorphosis—complete and incomplete.

Complete Metamorphosis

In **complete metamorphosis**, an insect's body changes *completely* from egg to adult. There are four stages in complete metamorphosis.

Adult—the reproductive stage of the insect. Adult insects often have wings. In many insects, the adult stage is relatively short. Adults often eat very different foods from the larvae. Some insects do not eat as adults.

Egg—contains the embryo of the new insect.

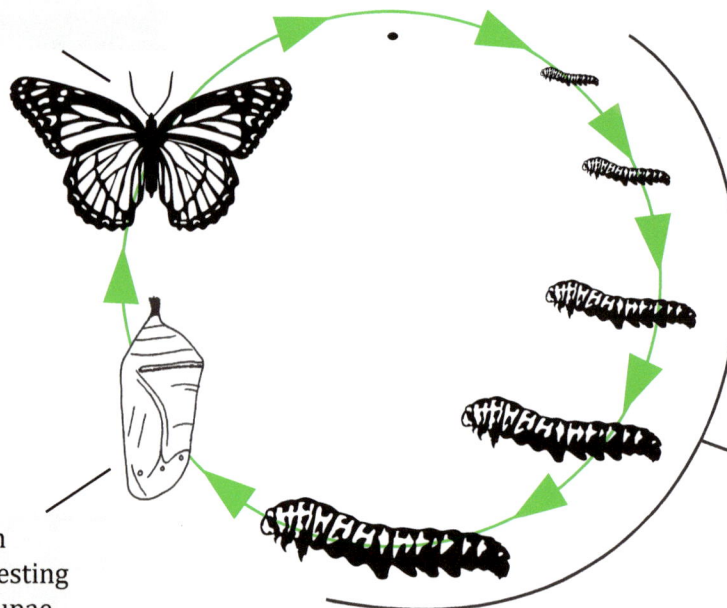

Pupa—this is often described as the "resting stage", because a pupae don't move much. It looks like nothing is happening, but inside the pupa, the insect's body is changing a lot.

Larva—the young stage. This stage is focused on growth. It goes through several **instars**, or stages of growth between moulting. Most insects spend the majority of their lives as a larva.

Examples of insects that go through complete metamorphosis are bees, wasps, ants, butterflies, moths, beetles, and flies.

Incomplete Metamorphosis

Incomplete metamorphosis is a simpler change than complete metamorphosis. There are only three stages.

Adult—the reproductive stage of the insect. Adult insects often have wings. In insects that go through incomplete metamorphosis, nymphs and adults usually eat the same foods.

Egg—contains the embryo of the new insect.

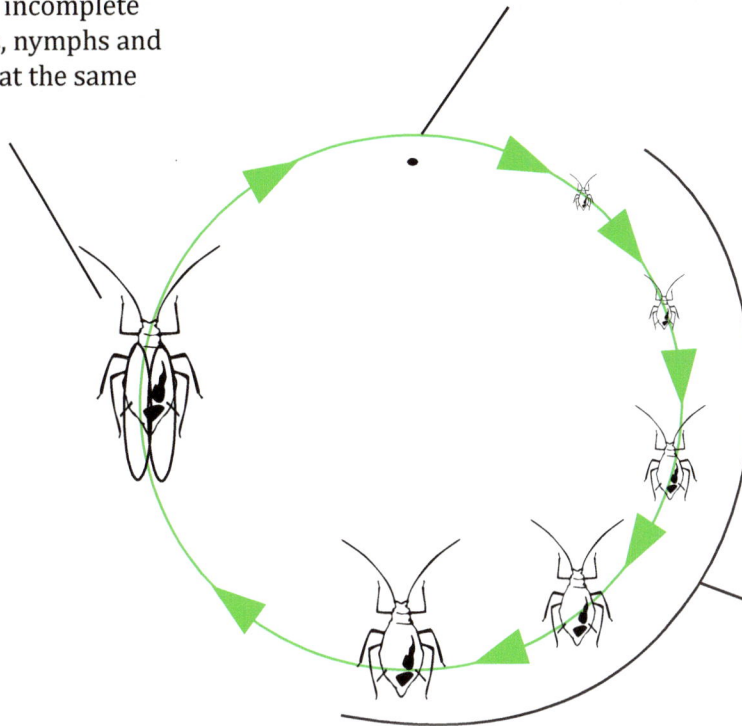

Nymph—the young stage. The nymph looks much like a miniature adult without wings. This stage is focused on growth and goes through several instars. Each instar looks more and more like the adult insect. Nymphs have wing buds that get larger in each instar.

Examples of insects that go through incomplete metamorphosis are grasshoppers, crickets, wētā, cicadas, aphids, stick insects, and praying mantids.

Growth and Moulting

An insect's exoskeleton does not grow once it has formed and hardened. For an insect to get bigger, it needs to shed its exoskeleton and grow a larger one (a bit like children who need new clothes as they grow out of their old ones). We call this process **moulting**.

When an insect moults, it finds a safe spot where it is protected from weather and predators. Its old exoskeleton splits down the back, and the insect crawls out of it.

The new exoskeleton has formed underneath the old, but when the insect first emerges from the old exoskeleton, the new one is pale, soft, and flexible. The insect expands the new exoskeleton while it is soft, often by gulping air or water. As the exoskeleton hardens, it darkens. Until the exoskeleton is hard, the insect can't move much (imagine if all your bones were soft instead of rigid), and is vulnerable to predators.

Other Arthropods

Many of the creatures you find in your backyard aren't insects, but are other **arthropods**. Below are a few of the more common ones. Photos and identification keys for these animals can be found in the Identifying Insects section.

Spiders

Spiders have eight legs, two main body regions (a **cephalothorax** and an abdomen), six or eight simple eyes, and no antennae. Spiders produce silk from **spinnerets** located on their abdomens. They use silk for prey capture, shelter, protecting their eggs, support and safety when climbing, and even for flying (a behaviour called **ballooning**). Almost all spiders are predators that subdue their prey with venom. There is only one herbivorous spider known.

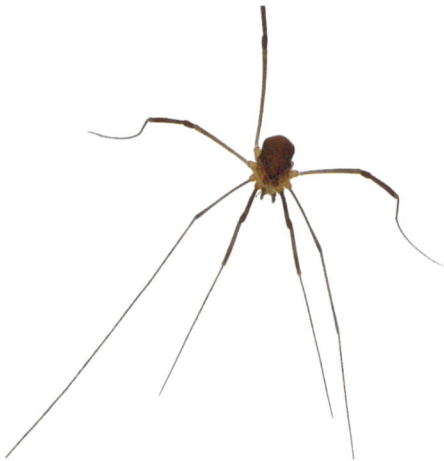

Harvestmen

Harvestmen are often confused with spiders, as they have eight legs and no antennae. They only have one major body region, however, not two like spiders. Harvestmen eat dead or very small insects. They have no venom and do not spin silk.

Slaters

Slaters are also known as isopods, woodlice, pill bugs, sow bugs, roly polies, potato bugs, and a host of other names. Slaters are crustaceans, related to crabs and crayfish. They have 12 or 14 legs on segmented bodies. They have two pairs of antennae, but only one pair is easily seen. Like all crustaceans, slaters breathe through gills. To survive on land, they carry water with them, surrounding their gills.

Millipedes

Millipedes have a long, rope-like, segmented body. They have 25 to 100 pairs of legs, which sit largely underneath the body. They are generally slow-moving, and often curl up when threatened. Millipedes are scavengers, eating mostly dead plants.

Centipedes

Centipedes have a long body like millipedes, but the body is flattened. Twenty-five to 100 pairs of legs stick out from the sides of the body. Centipedes are fast-moving and usually run when disturbed. They are predators on other invertebrates, and their first pair of legs is modified into poison fangs. Larger centipedes can give a sharp bite if handled roughly.

Ticks and Mites

Ticks and mites have two main body regions, but they often appear as one. They have eight short legs (six when newly hatched), and no antennae. Most are very small. They are a highly diverse group of arthropods including parasites, predators, and herbivores.

Hoppers

Hoppers are crustaceans, and look a lot like shrimp (though they live on land). They rarely sit still for identification, but are known by their behaviour—springing frantically away when disturbed. Sand hoppers are common on the beach, and land hoppers can often be found in moist areas under logs.

Pseudoscorpions

These tiny arthropods are common in leaf litter, but are seldom seen. They resemble a miniature scorpion without a tail. Their two large pincers are used for grabbing the dead leaves they eat.

Photos: millipede--Eiten F., mite--Olaf Leillinger, hopper--US National Park Service, Oregon Caves National Park, pseudoscorpion--public domain

Insect Classification

Many people lump all creepy-crawlies into one category—bugs. That informal category can include animals as diverse as worms, spiders, insects, centipedes, and slaters. Unfortunately, the category is meaningless if we're trying to make sense of what "bugs" are, and how they're related. For example, earthworms are in the phylum Annelida, insects are in the phylum Arthropoda, and humans are in the phylum Chordata, all within the kingdom Animalia.

By this measure, we are as likely as insects and worms to be "bugs."

The figure on the following page includes most of the familiar creepy-crawlies, giving you an idea of their **taxonomy** and diversity.

Many of these creatures are included in the keys in the Identifying Insects section.

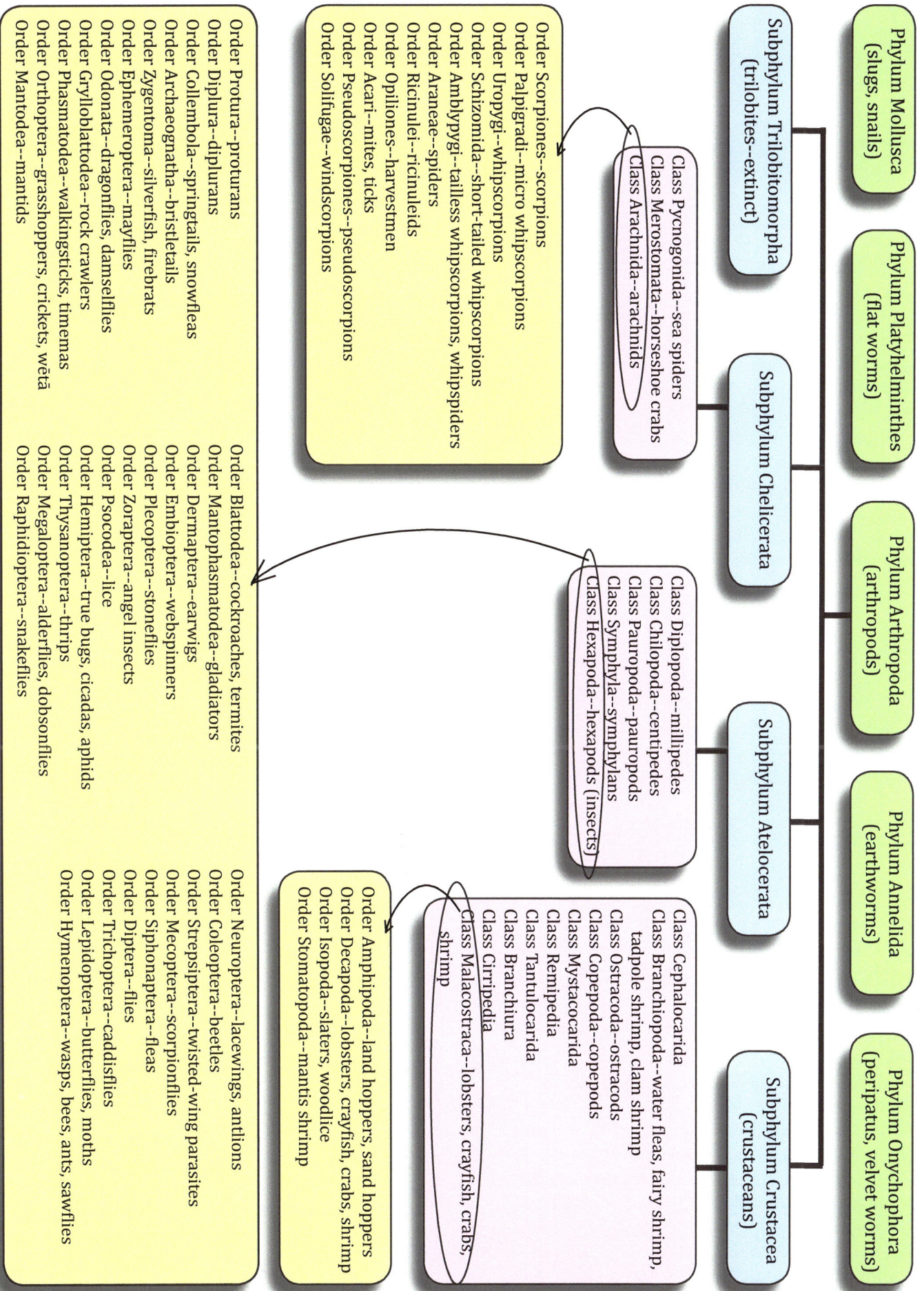

Phylum Mollusca (slugs, snails)

Phylum Platyhelminthes (flat worms)

Phylum Arthropoda (arthropods)

- **Subphylum Trilobitomorpha** (trilobites--extinct)

- **Subphylum Chelicerata**
  - Class Pycnogonida--sea spiders
  - Class Merostomata--horseshoe crabs
  - Class Arachnida--arachnids
    - Order Scorpiones--scorpions
    - Order Palpigradi--micro whipscorpions
    - Order Uropygi--whipscorpions
    - Order Schizomida--short-tailed whipscorpions
    - Order Amblypygi--tailless whipscorpions, whipspiders
    - Order Araneae--spiders
    - Order Ricinulei--ricinuleids
    - Order Opiliones--harvestmen
    - Order Acari--mites, ticks
    - Order Pseudoscorpiones--pseudoscorpions
    - Order Solifugae--windscorpions

- **Subphylum Atelocerata**
  - Class Diplopoda--millipedes
  - Class Chilopoda--centipedes
  - Class Pauropoda--pauropods
  - Class Symphyla--symphylans
  - Class Hexapoda--hexapods (insects)
    - Order Protura--proturans
    - Order Diplura--diplurans
    - Order Collembola--springtails, snowfleas
    - Order Archaeognatha--bristletails
    - Order Zygentoma--silverfish, firebrats
    - Order Ephemeroptera--mayflies
    - Order Odonata--dragonflies, damselflies
    - Order Grylloblattodea--rock crawlers
    - Order Phasmatodea--walkingsticks, timemas
    - Order Orthoptera--grasshoppers, crickets, wētā
    - Order Mantodea--mantids
    - Order Blattodea--cockroaches, termites
    - Order Mantophasmatodea--gladiators
    - Order Dermaptera--earwigs
    - Order Embioptera--webspinners
    - Order Plecoptera--stoneflies
    - Order Zoraptera--angel insects
    - Order Psocodea--lice
    - Order Hemiptera--true bugs, cicadas, aphids
    - Order Thysanoptera--thrips
    - Order Megaloptera--alderflies, dobsonflies
    - Order Raphidioptera--snakeflies
    - Order Neuroptera--lacewings, antlions
    - Order Coleoptera--beetles
    - Order Strepsiptera--twisted-wing parasites
    - Order Mecoptera--scorpionflies
    - Order Siphonaptera--fleas
    - Order Diptera--flies
    - Order Trichoptera--caddisflies
    - Order Lepidoptera--butterflies, moths
    - Order Hymenoptera--wasps, bees, ants, sawflies

- **Subphylum Crustacea** (crustaceans)
  - Class Cephalocarida
  - Class Branchiopoda--water fleas, fairy shrimp, tadpole shrimp, clam shrimp
  - Class Ostracoda--ostracods
  - Class Copepoda--copepods
  - Class Mystacocarida
  - Class Remipedia
  - Class Tantulocarida
  - Class Branchiura
  - Class Cirripedia
  - Class Malacostraca--lobsters, crayfish, crabs, shrimp
    - Order Amphipoda--land hoppers, sand hoppers
    - Order Decapoda--lobsters, crayfish, crabs, shrimp
    - Order Isopoda--slaters, woodlice
    - Order Stomatopoda--mantis shrimp

Phylum Annelida (earthworms)

Phylum Onychophora (peripatus, velvet worms)

Why Are Insects Important?

Insects matter. Without them we humans (and most other vertebrates) couldn't survive. Here are just a few of the ways insects are important to us.

Natural Ecology

Insects are essential parts of terrestrial ecosystems. They perform roles as pollinators, decomposers, predators, and prey. Their sheer numbers reflect their importance in natural systems. There are nearly a million species of insect described by scientists, and up to 7.8 million as yet undiscovered species (compare that with about 4,000 mammalian species). There are an estimated 200 million insects per person on earth. And lest you think that because they're small their numbers don't amount to much, one study found that a third of the animal biomass in the Amazon rainforest is made up of just ants and termites.

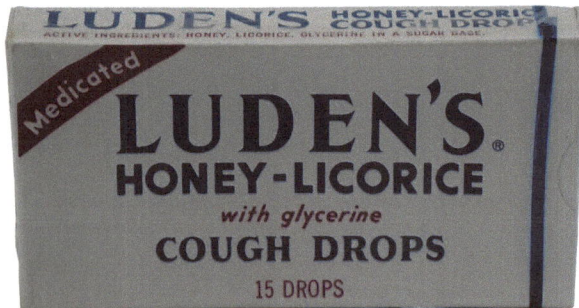

Photo: Andrew Filer

Medicine

Insects and their products have been used in folk medicine for centuries. Even in today's modern medicine, insects have a place. Blow fly larvae are sometimes used to clean wounds, as they eat only dead flesh, and excrete allantoin, which promotes healing, leaving a wound clean and better able to heal. Honey's antimicrobial properties are also used to help heal wounds. Honey and beeswax are used to treat a variety of skin disorders. Bee and ant venom are used to treat arthritis. Beeswax has been used to create slow-release drug capsules. Extracts from blister beetles have shown promise against cancer in the laboratory, and more insect products are tested every day for medicinal properties.

Agriculture

Human agriculture is intimately linked with insects. Pest insects threaten crops and livestock; beneficial insects help keep pests and weeds in check; and bees and other insects pollinate fruits and vegetables. According to Apiculture New Zealand, the value of honeybees alone in New Zealand is over $3 billion annually. This includes the $48.2 million per year beekeeping industry, pollination of pasture legumes, and crop pollination. If insects were to suddenly vanish, much of our food and fibre production would vanish along with them.

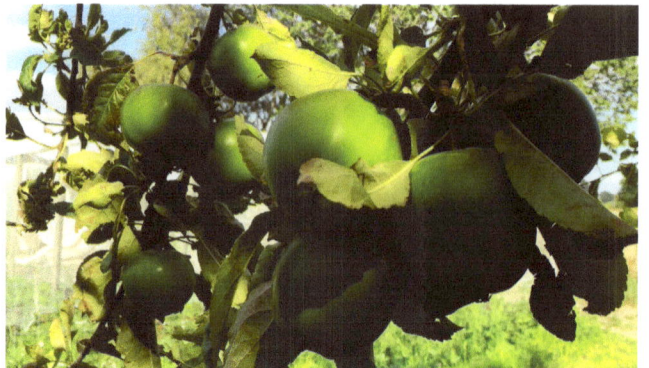

Food

In most human societies, insects provide an important source of nutrition. High in protein and essential nutrients like iron and calcium, insects provide up to 10% of the animal protein in some people's diets. In New Zealand today, **entomophagy** (insect eating) is limited to a novelty at the Wild Foods Festival and at some restaurants. The traditional Māori diet, however, included a variety of insects, some of which are considered pests today.

Though New Zealanders don't often knowingly eat insects today, there are plenty of insects and insect-derived products on the supermarket shelves. Honey is the obvious one, but there are others.

The red food dye, carmine, also known as cochineal, is sold as a food colouring and is used in a variety of products, from fruit juice to candy to cosmetics. This dye is made from the bodies of the cochineal scale insect (*Dactylopius coccus*).

Another insect product in our food is shellac. Shellac is produced by the lac insect, *Laccifer lacca*. It is used to add gloss to candies and fresh fruit. It is also used as a wood and leather finish, as a coating on pills, as a dye, in printer ink, in cosmetics, and in a wide range of other manufactured goods.

Silk

About 32 million kilograms of silk are produced each year and are woven into high-value textiles. Silk is produced by the caterpillar of the moth *Bombyx mori*.

Inviting Insects To Your Yard

Planting an insect garden is a great way to invite arthropods to your yard. I use the term "insect" for simplicity, but a good "insect" garden will attract spiders, centipedes, millipedes, and slaters as well.

Like all animals, insects need food, water, and shelter to survive. An insect garden must provide all these things in order to attract insects.

Food

Flowering plants for nectar and pollen—Many insects eat nectar or pollen as adults. Providing year-round flowers of the right type will attract a wide variety of flies, butterflies, beetles, beneficial wasps, and bees to the garden. Choose plants with small, flat, open flowers, which provide the best access to nectar. Choose a mix of plants so that you have year-round flowers.

Some particularly good insect-attracting flowers are:

Coriander
Dill
Fennel
Mint
Lemon balm
Oregano
Rosemary
Sunflowers
Scabiosa
Daisies
Yarrow
Cosmos
Chamomile

Food for predatory insects—You can see some exciting predator/prey interactions if your garden provides plenty of food for predators. Plant lettuces, cabbage and broccoli to encourage aphids, white butterfly caterpillars, and slugs that will attract a variety of predators and parasites.

Water

Though many insects get the water they need from their food, some appreciate a shallow dish of water with a wide lip, or a small puddle, particularly on hot dry days.

Shelter

Encourage insects to settle down and reproduce in your garden by providing shelter from predators and the elements. Shelter should include:

- Logs, rocks, overturned flowerpots, or stacks of bricks.
- Plants of varied heights, including some dense groundcovers.
- Shady spots.

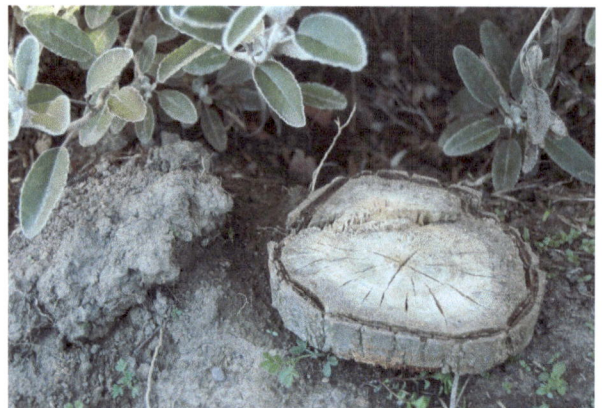

Other Attractants

Sunning spots—Many insects like sunny places for warming up in the morning. Set a large rock in a sunny spot or incorporate a sunny wall of a building into your insect garden.

Puddling spots—A puddle or patch of mud can attract butterflies who "puddle", sucking up the mineral-laden moisture from the soil.

Mānuka and kānuka—If stick insects are present in your neighbourhood, mānuka and kānuka can attract them to your yard.

Ake ake—Katydids love this tree. Listen for their late afternoon "zit!" call.

Long grass—Crickets prefer long grass and will set up house in an unmowed corner of your yard.

Swan plant—This plant will attract monarch butterflies, as it is the only food plant for their caterpillars. Be aware, however, that the plant is poisonous.

Caring for Insects in Captivity

Mealworm

Mealworms can be purchased from pet shops and live insect suppliers (see Resources section). To raise mealworms, put 5 to 10 cm of wheat bran in the bottom of a plastic pan. Add 25 to 50 beetles, and place a small slice of potato on top of the meal for moisture. Replace the potato whenever it dries out or becomes mouldy.

The beetles start laying eggs 7 to 10 days after emergence, and the eggs hatch about 14 days later. The time spent in the larval stage varies with temperature and food availability. The larvae grow rapidly under ideal conditions until they are about 25 mm long, then they pupate. The adults emerge 2 to 3 weeks after pupation.

Praying Mantis

New Zealand praying mantis eggs are deposited on branches, tree trunks, fence posts, and walls in the fall in a greyish foam case with a white "plait" down the front. The egg case overwinters, and the young hatch in the spring and mature through summer.

Each egg case contains up to 70 eggs. Collect egg cases in late winter by clipping the branch to which they are attached and placing it in an aquarium or jar. Observe the eggs daily to watch for emerging mantids.

Praying mantids are cannibalistic and must be housed individually or in a very large aquarium with lots of vegetation so the mantids can hide from one another. A small jar can be used for young mantids. A thin cloth secured with an elastic band makes a good lid, and a small stick will provide a roost for the young insect.

Praying mantids must be fed live insects. Fruit flies and aphids are excellent foods for young mantids. As the mantids grow, provide larger food (house flies and blow flies are good). Provide water by misting the cage every day or two.

Mealworm photo: Rasbak

Monarch Butterfly

Monarchs can be kept year round indoors. Collect caterpillars during the summer. Caterpillars can be kept on potted swan plants or cut swan plant branches. The plants need not be in a cage. To keep caterpillars from wandering, place the pot in a tray of water—the caterpillars will not cross the water.

When caterpillars pupate and emerge as adults, transfer them to a large cage. Feed them fresh flowers or a sugar solution made of 1 tablespoon of honey and a quarter-cup of water, refreshed daily. To feed sugar solution, place a small piece of sponge or a folded paper towel in a jar lid and soak with sugar solution.

Adults will lay small yellowish eggs on swan plants placed in the cage. You will need to have several potted swan plants to use as food for the emerging larvae. As the eggs hatch and the larvae grow, monitor the population carefully and cull caterpillars as needed so that they do not strip all your swan plants (kill excess caterpillars by placing in a container in the freezer). If you run out of swan plants, you can rear caterpillars on slices of fresh pumpkin. Pumpkin is not a natural food for monarchs, and caterpillars cannot complete their entire development on it—expect young ones to die. Older caterpillars will be able to complete their development, however.

Slater

Slaters can be collected from moist garden areas. There are two easily distinguishable groups of slaters—those that can curl into a hard ball (in the family Armadillidae), and those that can't curl up (in the families Oniscidae and Porcellionidae). Females of both groups carry eggs in a brood pouch. Development from young to adult usually takes about a year.

Slaters should be placed in a container (large jar, aquarium, bucket, or deep tray) with 2-3 cm of soil on the bottom. The soil should be kept moist, but not wet. Small pieces of wood can be added for the slaters to hide under. Feed them slices of potato and dead leaves.

Insect Cages

There are many ways to house insects. You don't need to spend a lot on an insect cage. An effective cage should contain the insects and maintain appropriate air flow, temperature, and humidity for them.

An empty jar makes a great cage for many insects. Cover the top with a piece of mesh or cloth, held on by an elastic band.

Inexpensive plastic aquaria come in many sizes and can be fitted out for most insects.

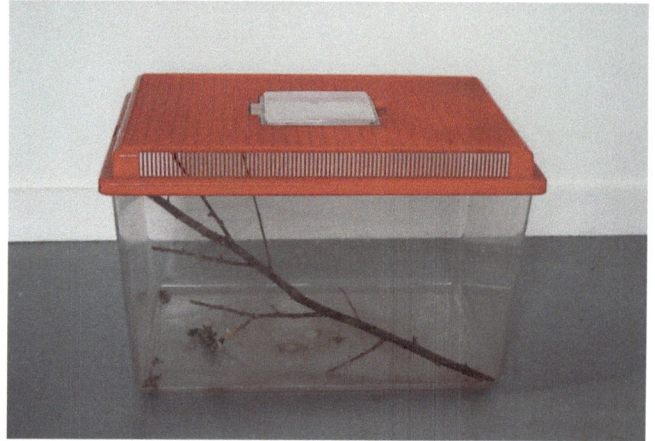

Soil insects can be housed in a juice bottle turned on its side and fitted with a mesh 'window'.

Tape mesh over a hole cut in the lid of a margarine tub to create a cage for non-flying insects.

Identifying Insects

When scientists identify arthropods, they often use keys. Keys allow you to answer simple questions about the animal you're trying to identify, and follow the answers to the correct identification.

On the following pages are two different keys to arthropods you might find in your back yard. They won't identify your creature to species, but will let you know what larger group your organism belongs in. With that information, it will be much easier to identify it to species.

Picture Key to Garden and Park Invertebrates: This key separates insects from other invertebrates you might find, like slugs, centipedes, and spiders.

Key to Common Garden and Park Insects in New Zealand: Once you know you have an insect, you can use this key to narrow down what sort of insect you have.

Picture Key to Garden and Park Invertebrates

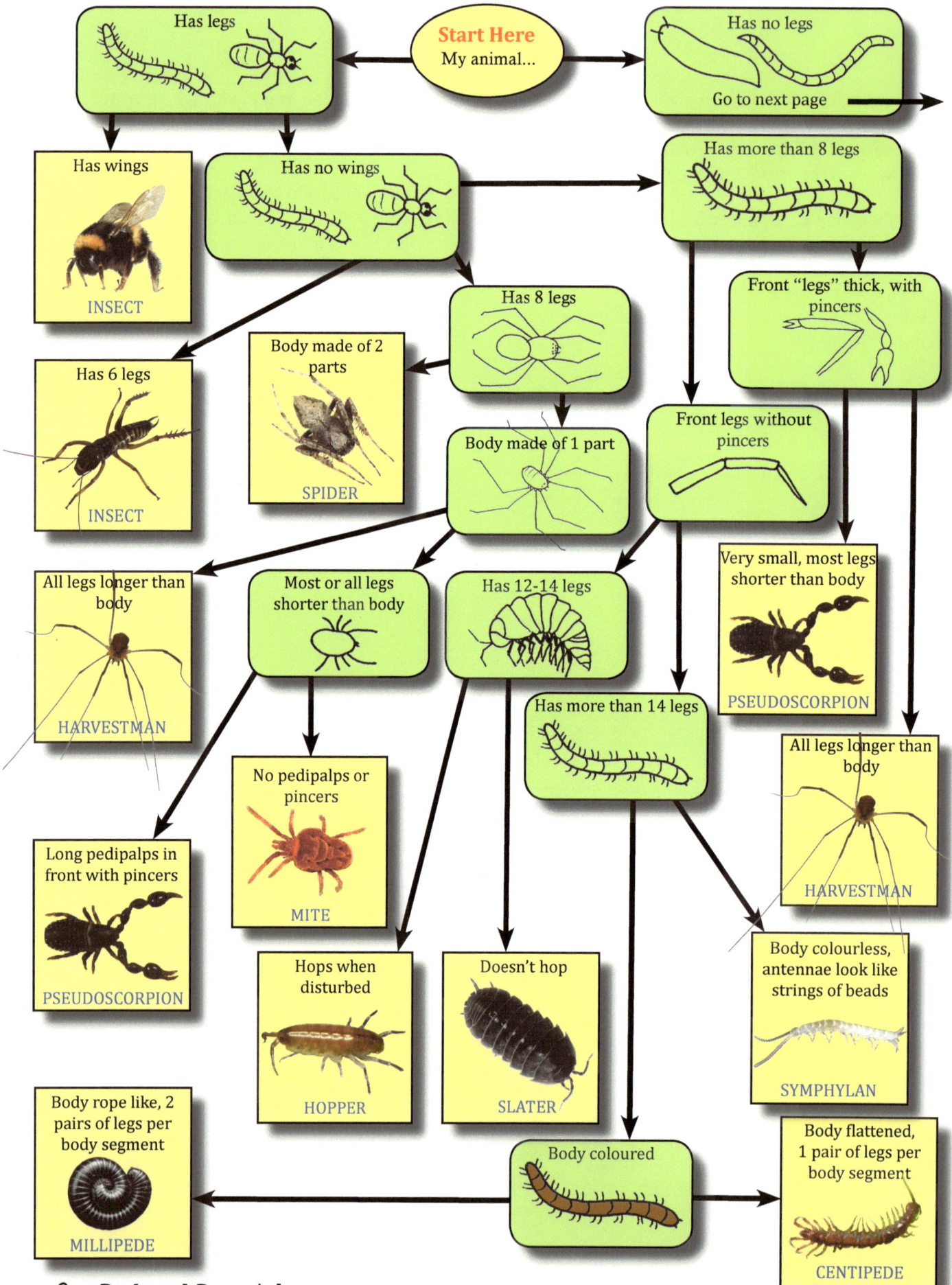

Start Here
My animal...

Has legs

Has no legs
Go to next page

Has wings
INSECT

Has no wings

Has more than 8 legs

Front "legs" thick, with pincers

Has 6 legs
INSECT

Body made of 2 parts
SPIDER

Has 8 legs

Front legs without pincers

All legs longer than body
HARVESTMAN

Most or all legs shorter than body

Body made of 1 part

Has 12-14 legs

Very small, most legs shorter than body
PSEUDOSCORPION

No pedipalps or pincers
MITE

Has more than 14 legs

All legs longer than body
HARVESTMAN

Long pedipalps in front with pincers
PSEUDOSCORPION

Hops when disturbed
HOPPER

Doesn't hop
SLATER

Body colourless, antennae look like strings of beads
SYMPHYLAN

Body rope like, 2 pairs of legs per body segment
MILLIPEDE

Body coloured

Body flattened, 1 pair of legs per body segment
CENTIPEDE

Start Here
Invertebrates without legs

Body made of segments

Body not made of segments

Has no shell

Body pink or brown, up to 15 cm long, no visible head

EARTHWORM

Has a shell

SNAIL

Body tiny (usually <2 mm), wormlike, usually white

NEMATODE

Body rounded, up to 3 cm long, grey or brown

SLUG

Body very flat, usually dark brown or orange

FLATWORM

Body usually white or tan, <6 cm long, head usually visible

INSECT LARVA

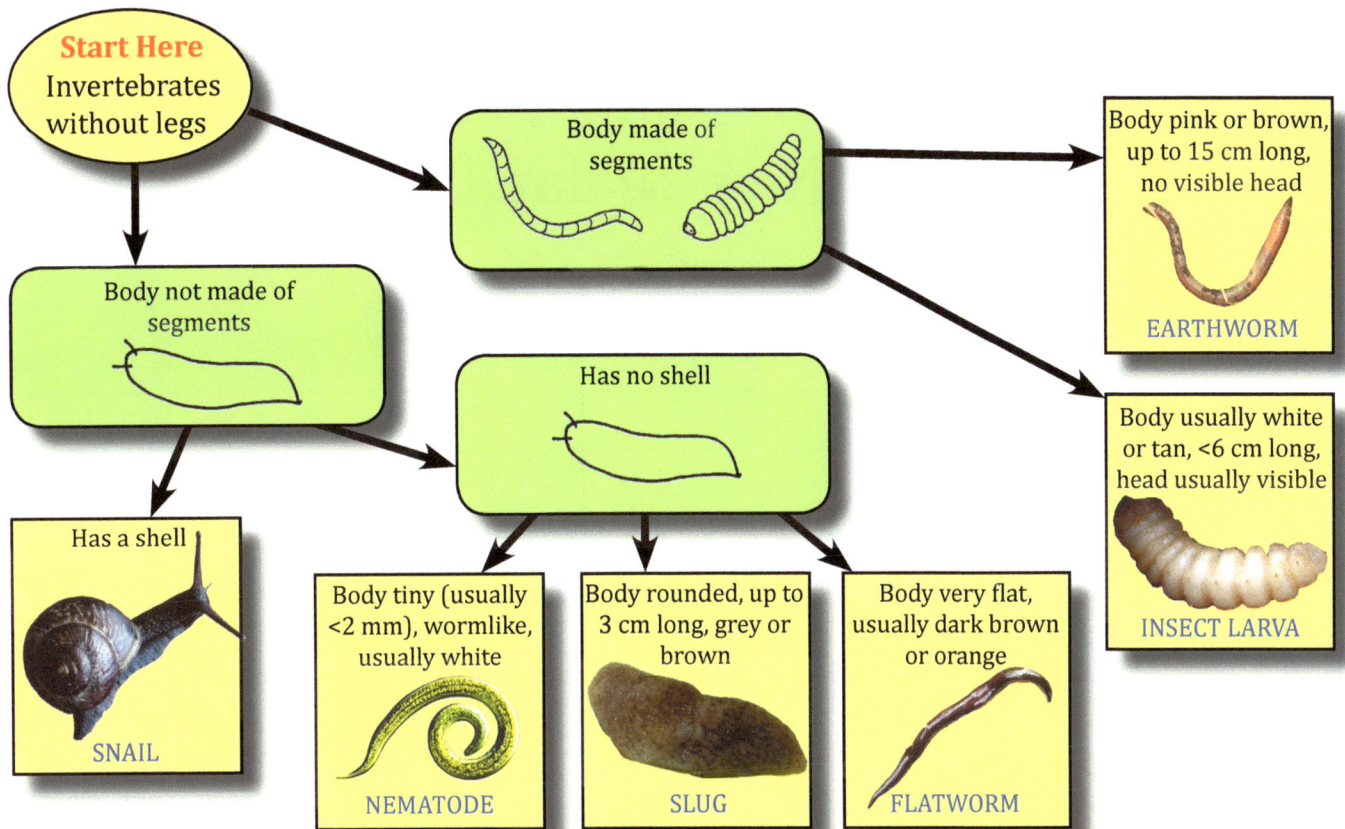

More About These Invertebrates

INSECTS have 6 legs, 2 antennae, and 3 main body parts. Most adult insects have wings. They are the only invertebrates with wings.

INSECT LARVAE come in many shapes, sizes, and colours. Some have legs, some don't. Insect larvae never have wings; only adults do.

SPIDERS have 8 legs, no antennae, and 2 main body parts. Spiders spin silk, and use poison fangs to paralyse their prey.

SNAILS and SLUGS have no legs. They move with a muscular "foot" that glides over a trail of slime. A snail's shell grows with it.

HARVESTMEN have 8 legs, no antennae, and 1 main body part. They do not spin silk, and do not have poison fangs.

NEMATODES are usually colourless and less than 2 mm long. There are millions of them in every shovelful of soil.

EARTHWORMS have no legs, and a long body made of segments. Most are less than 15 cm long, but some can reach 1.5 metres.

CENTIPEDES and MILLIPEDES may look similar, but they live very different lives. Millipedes are scavengers, eating mostly dead plants. Centipedes are predators that kill other invertebrates with poison fangs.

Photos: Snail--Hakan Svensson; Symphylan--Sonia Martinez; Insect Larva--Charlotte Simmonds; Mite--Olaf Leillinger; Millipede--Eiten F; Nematode--CSIRO; Hopper--US National Park Service, Oregon Caves National Park; Flatworm and Pseudoscorpion--public domain; all other photos--Robinne Weiss

Key to Common Garden and Park Insects in New Zealand

(adult insects only)

1	a	has wings	go to #2
	b	has no wings	go to #3
2	a	has 1 pair of wings	Diptera (flies)
	b	has 2 pairs wings	go to #4
3	a	jumps	Orthoptera (grasshoppers, crickets, weta)
	b	doesn't jump	go to #6
4	a	front wings form a hard shell	Coleoptera (beetles)
	b	front wings don't form a shell	go to #9
5	a	pincers at the end of the abdomen	Dermaptera (earwigs; actually have wings, but not usually visible)
	b	no pincers at the end of the abdomen	go to #6
6	a	body long and stick-like	Phasmatodea (stick insects)
	b	body not shaped like a stick	go to #7
7	a	body rounded, often green or grey, found on plants	Hemiptera (aphids)
	b	body has a 'waist', dark coloured, often found on the ground	Hymenoptera (ants)
8	a	wings covered in scales	Lepidoptera (butterflies, moths)
	b	wings clear, membranous	go to #9

9	a	mouthparts straw-like (piercing-sucking)	Hemiptera (plant hoppers, cicadas, aphids, true bugs)
	b	mouthparts not straw-like	go to #10
10	a	large pincers at end of abdomen	Dermaptera (earwigs)
	b	no pincers at end of abdomen	go to #11
11	a	wings showy	go to #12
	b	wings not showy, held flat against back	go to #13
12	a	usually found near water, strong fliers	Odonata (dragonflies, damselflies)
	b	often found near flowers, may have warning colouration	Hymenoptera (bees, wasps, ants)
13	a	body flattened	Blattodea (cockroaches)
	b	body not flattened	go to #14
14	a	front legs enlarged for capturing prey (raptorial)	Mantodea (mantids)
	b	back legs enlarged for jumping (saltatorial)	Orthoptera (grasshoppers)

Resources

Books

NZ-specific:

A Mini Guide to the Identification of New Zealand Insects (Andrew Crowe; Penguin, 2010)

Stick Insects (NZ Wild) (Steve Trewick and Mary Morgan-Richards; Raupo Publishing, 2005)

The Life-Size Guide to Insects and Other Land Invertebrates of New Zealand (Andrew Crowe; Penguin Books, 1999)

All About New Zealand's Garden Wildlife (Dave Gunson; New Holland Publishers, 2012)

The Monarch Butterfly in New Zealand (George Gibbs; Entomological Society of New Zealand, 2013)

New Zealand Garden Wildlife to Read, Colour and Keep (Dave Gunson; New Holland Publishing, 2012)

An Illustrated Guide to Some New Zealand Insect Families (Elizabeth A. Grant; Manaaki Whenua Press, 1999)

Butterflies and Moths of New Zealand (Brian Parkinson and Brian Patrick; Reed Books, 2000)

Managing Pests and Diseases: a Handbook for New Zealand Gardeners (Rob Lucas; Craig Potton Publishing, 2005)

Which New Zealand Insect? (Andrew Crowe; Penguin Books, 2002)

Which New Zealand Spider? (Andrew Crowe; Penguin Books, 2007)

Spiders of New Zealand and their Worldwide Kin (Ray Forster and Lyn Forster; University of Otago Press, 1999)

New Zealand Weta (George Gibbs; Reed Books, 1998)

The Weta Book: A guide to the identification of wetas (Mike Meads; Manaaki Whenua Press, 1990)

Keeping Wetas in Captivity (Paul Barrett, ed. G.W. Ramsay; Wellington Zoological Gardens, 1991)

Life-Size Guide to New Zealand Native Ferns: featuring the unique caterpillars which feed on them (Andrew Crowe; Penguin Books, 2004)

A Photographic Guide to Insects of New Zealand (Brian Parkinson and Don Horne; New Holland Publishers, 2007)

Biological Control Agents for Weeds in New Zealand: a field guide (Lynley Hayes; Landcare Research New Zealand, Ltd, 2005; available as a free pdf at: https://www.landcareresearch.co.nz/__data/assets/pdf_file/0019/43138/weeds_field_guide.pdf)

General Entomology:

The Practical Entomologist: an Introductory Guide to Observing and Understanding the World of Insects (Rick Imes; Simon and Schuster Inc, 1992)

The Insects: an Outline of Entomology, 4th Edition (P.J. Gullan and P.S. Cranston; John Wiley & Sons Ltd, 2010)

Bugs in the System: Insects and Their Impact on Human Affairs (May R. Berenbaum; Addison-Wesley Publishing Company Inc., 1995)

Spineless Wonders: Strange Tales from the Invertebrate World (Richard Conniff; Henry Holt and Company, 1996)

Man Eating Bugs: The Art and Science of Eating Insects (Peter Menzel and Faith D'Aluiso; Material World, 1998)

Educational Resources

Science Resource Box--http://scienceresourcebox.co.nz/information/information&information_id=7
Bug Wise: Thirty Incredible Insect Investigations and Arachnid Activities (Pamela M. Hickman; Addison-Wesley Publishing Company Inc, 1990)
Insects and Spiders: Mind-boggling Experiments You Can Turn into Science Fair Projects (Janice VanCleave; John Wiley and Sons Inc, 1998)
Bug Camp: Where Every Day's an Adventure (Tim Forrest and Jen Hamel; Moon Dance Press, 2016)

Online Resources

NZ-based:
Landcare Research Insects and Spiders Resources--http://www.landcareresearch.co.nz/resources/teaching/Insects-and-spiders
Te Papa Spiders of New Zealand Teaching Resources--https://www.tepapa.govt.nz/learn/for-educators/teaching-resources/spiders-new-zealand-teaching-resource

Entomological Society of New Zealand--http://ento.org.nz/
Apiculture New Zealand--http://apinz.org.nz/

International:
The Pennsylvania State University Department of Entomology, Education and Outreach--http://ento.psu.edu/public
Iowa State Entomology Index of Internet Resources--http://www.ent.iastate.edu/list/directory/158/vid/5
Texas A&M University Agrilife Extension--http://www.texasinsects.org/

Entomological suppliers

BioQuip Products--http://www.bioquip.com/
Australian Entomological Supplies--http://www.entosupplies.com.au/
Biosuppliers (live insects)--http://biosuppliers.nz/
Zonda (live insects)--http://www.zonda.net.nz/
Insects Direct (live crickets)--http://www.insectdirect.co.nz/

Citizen Science

NatureWatch NZ, where anyone can record observations of nature, and engage with scientists--http://naturewatch.org.nz/

Glossary

Abdomen	The rearmost region of an insect or spider's body. Houses reproductive, respiratory, and digestive organs.
Antenna (plural, antennae)	Sensory organs attached to the head of insects and some other arthropods. Used for smell, feel, taste, and hearing.
Arthropod	A phylum of organisms with exoskeletons and jointed legs.
Ballooning	A type of locomotion in which a young spider spins a thread of silk and allows the wind to blow it away, carrying the spider with it.
Biodiversity	The diversity of life. All the living things in a particular place.
Camouflage	Hiding by looking like the background.
Cephalothorax	The front body region of a spider. Eyes, mouthparts, pedipalps, and legs are all attached here.
Cerci	Sensory appendages on the tip of an insect's abdomen.
Classification	The organisation of living things into groups, such as kingdom, phylum, class, order, family, genus, and species.
Compound eye	A cluster of simple eyes (ommatidia).
Entomophagy	Eating insects.
Exoskeleton	A skeleton on the outside of the body.
Ganglion (plural, ganglia)	A cluster of nerve cells that acts like a mini-brain.
Habitat	An area in which an organism lives.
Head	The front body region of an insect. Eyes, mouthparts, and antennae are attached here.
Hemolymph	Insect 'blood'. Carries nutrients, hormones, and immune defences, but usually not oxygen.
Instar	A stage of insect growth between moults.
Larva (plural, larvae)	The immature phase of an insect that undergoes complete metamorphosis.
Mandibles	An insect's 'jaws'. In chewing-type mouthparts, mandibles are used for grasping and tearing apart food.
Metamorphosis	A change in body shape over an animal's lifetime.
Moulting	Shedding the exoskeleton.
Nymph	The immature phase of an insect that undergoes incomplete metamorphosis.
Ocellus (plural, ocelli)	Simple eyes of insects. Most insects have three located in a triangle on the top of the head. Ocelli are involved in regulating the insect's diurnal schedule.

Ommatidium (plural, ommatidia)	A single unit of an insect's compound eye.
Ovipositor	Egg-laying tube, usually on the tip of the abdomen. Common in wasps, crickets, wētā, and grasshoppers.
Pedipalp	A sensory appendage of a spider, attached to the cephalothorax.
Phylogeny	The evolutionary history of an organism.
Pollination	The transfer of pollen from one flower to another for fertilisation.
Pupa (plural, pupae)	A stage of complete metamorphosis in which the insect's body changes dramatically from the larval form to the adult form.
Spinnerets	Silk-producing organ on the tip of a spider's abdomen.
Spiracle	A hole in an insect's body that allows air into the respiratory system.
Taxonomy	The naming and classification of organisms.
Thorax	Middle body region of an insect. Legs and wings are attached here.
Trachea	Branching tubes through an insect's body that carry oxygen to cells.

About the Author

I have been teaching about insects and other aspects of the natural world for over 25 years and have a Master's degree in Entomology.

Upon moving to New Zealand, I started The Bugmobile, delivering science outreach programmes with live insects to schools and preschools throughout Canterbury.

Today, I write full-time, spinning tales for children and young adults and blogging about rural life.

Visit me on-line at: robinneweiss.com

Also by Robinne Weiss

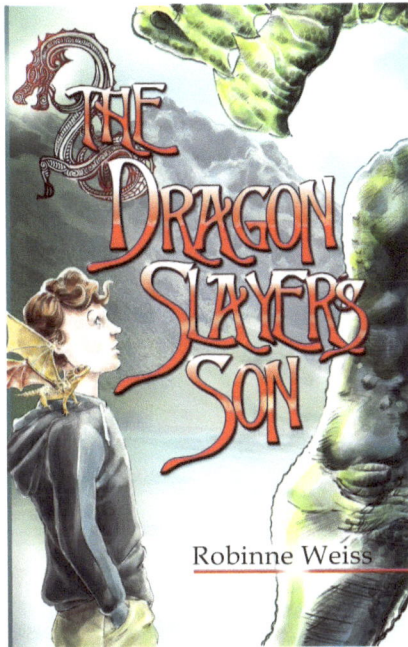

The Dragon Slayer's Son

Four friends, a missing dad, and dragons. A New Zealand adventure for ages 8-13.

A Glint of Exoskeleton

Can Crick and her cockroach sidekick foil the mosquitoes' plan to wipe out humans? A tropical adventure for ages 8-12.

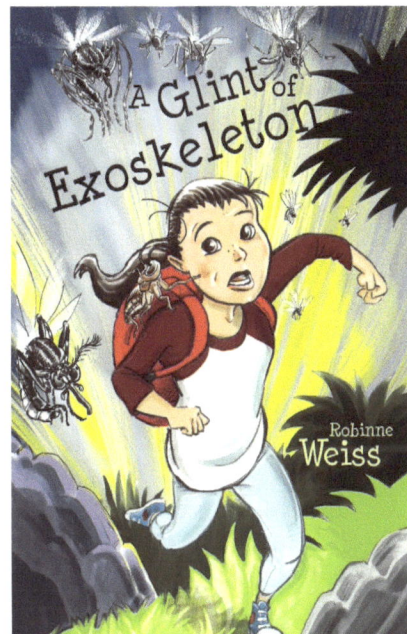

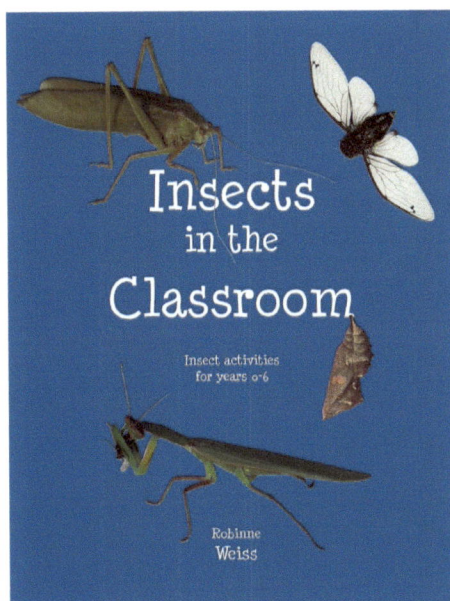

Insects in the Classroom

Drive your students buggy with classroom activities for years 0-6.

www.ingramcontent.com/pod-product-compliance
Lightning Source LLC
Chambersburg PA
CBHW060827270326
41931CB00002B/93